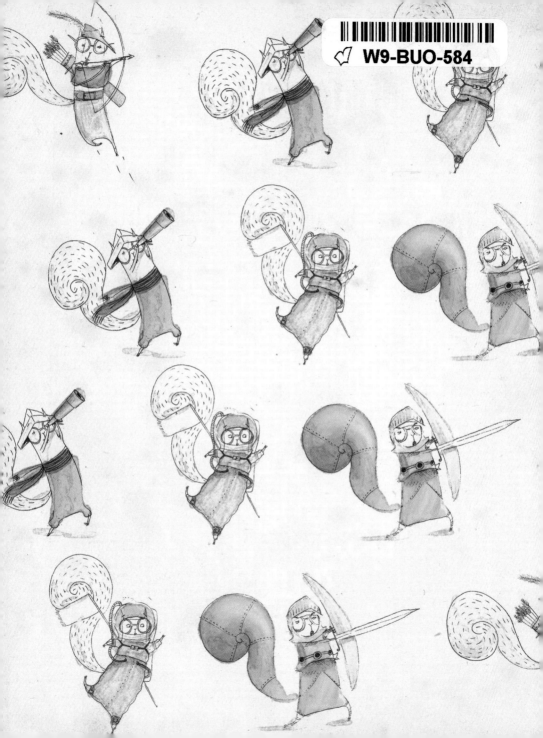

Alby's AMAZING BOOK

illustrated by
CATALINA ECHEVERRI

Some squirrels like
going on treasure hunts...

53

Some like
throwing acorns,

or playing chase.

But Alby likes
STORIES best of all!

You see, Alby doesn't just
read the **words,** or
look at the **pictures...**

Stories take him on amazing **ADVENTURES!**

Alby likes all sorts
of stories from all
sorts of books...

ACORN
LiBRaRY

OPEN

But his **favourite**
stories are all in one

very **SPECIAL** book.

It has stories about **GIANTS,**

stories about **RESCUES,**

even stories about

great big outer space!

With his special story book
there's **NOTHING** Alby can't do.

我唔明白

मैं समझा नहीं

ıๆ ɔıʋɑʋ

ন্যান শোন

わかりません

And **NOWHERE** he can't go!

You see...
there is something else that
makes this special book

extra,
EXTRA
SPECIAL...

Alby **KNOWS** the
person who wrote it!

holy
BIBLE

And he knows that these
stories aren't made up —

they are all **TRUE!**

Alby **LOVES** stories,
and he **LOVES** going
on adventures,

Because Alby knows that the One
who wrote his special book....

Loves him too!

ACORN LIBRARY
GOLD MEMBER
Name

thegoodbook
for children

Alby's Amazing Book
© Catalina Echeverri / The Good Book Company 2014.
This story is based on an original work by Mary Elizabeth Blume

'The Good Book For Children' is an imprint of The Good Book Company Ltd
Tel: 0333 123 0880; International: +44 (0) 208 942 0880 Email: info@thegoodbook.co.uk

Websites
UK: www.thegoodbook.co.uk   North America: www.thegoodbook.com
Australia: www.thegoodbook.com.au   New Zealand: www.thegoodbook.co.nz

Illustrated by Catalina Echeverri Design by André Parker
ISBN: 9781910307106 Printed by Proost Industries NV. Belgium

Scan here for a message
from the illustrator